A GROWTH MINDSET JOURNAL FOR STUDENTS
Grades 4-8

Love MATH JOURNAL

250+ QUICK PROMPTS, AFFIRMATIONS, AND REFLECTIONS TO CULTIVATE GRATITUDE, GROWTH MINDSET, AND A LOVE OF MATH.

Allison Dillard
Nicole Thomson

Copyright © 2021 Happy Hypotenuse Publishing

All rights reserved. No part of this publication may be reproduced, distributed, or transmitted in any form or by any means, including photocopying, recording, or other electronic or mechanical methods, without the prior written permission of the publisher, except in the case of brief quotations embodied in critical reviews and certain other noncommercial uses permitted by copyright law.

Published by:
Happy Hypotenuse Publishing, LLC
Mission Viejo, CA 92691

To contact the authors, please email:
allison@allisonlovesmath.com

Love Math Journal: 250+ Quick Prompts, Affirmations, and Reflections to Cultivate Gratitude, Growth Mindset, and a Love of Math.

Print ISBN: 978-1-950720-08-8

Love Math Journal

250+ Quick Prompts, Affirmations, and Reflections to Cultivate Gratitude, Growth Mindset, and a Love of Math

This journal belongs to

_____

FREE Guide for Teachers and Parents

For a quick, step-by-step guide to introduce this resource to your class or children, go to www.allisonlovesmath.com/journal

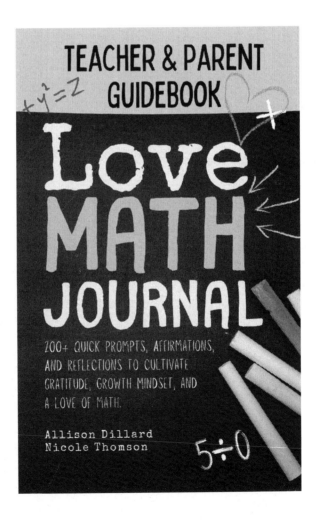

Dear Parents and Teachers,

We created the Love Math Journal to help your children and students build confidence and a passion for learning math and other challenges.

The Love Math Journal encourages curiosity and excitement about math, while strengthening social-emotional learning (SEL) skills, such as:
- identifying and managing emotions,
- recognizing sources of stress,
- learning to cope with challenges,
- maintaining motivation and perseverance,
- developing a sense of awareness,
- thinking critically and creatively,
- and cultivating a growth mindset toward math.

It also incorporates gratitude because students who practice gratitude regularly are better able to communicate, make decisions, solve problems, deal with anxiety, and work well with others - all things that benefit math students!

We designed the journal for you to be quick and easy to use. By spending 2-3 minutes actively nurturing your students' and children's mindsets and feelings toward math, you will help set them up for success. For a quick, step-by-step guide on how to introduce the journal to your class or children, go to www.allisonlovesmath.com/journal.

Happy journaling!

With gratitude,

Allison and Nicole

Dear Student,

Math will elevate your whole life. If you look deeply enough, math is in everything. Math will help you if you want to become an artist, a videogame designer, a baker, or work on special effects in movies. You need math to understand the data and analytics that will help your YouTube channel, Instagram following, or business succeed. Math will also help you make time for friends, budget and save money for fun trips, and even find the best price for a car.

Understanding the value math plays in your life will set you up for success in so many things beyond your math class. It teaches you how to tackle hard challenges, pick yourself up when you fall, and think outside-the-box to figure out how to accomplish the intimidating, yet inspiring, things you'd like to do.

What big, wild, amazing goals do you want to accomplish in your life? What big, wild, amazing difference do you want to make in the world? What big, wild, amazing life would you be proud to live? Whatever your answers are, math will help you get there. Whatever your dreams are, math will help you accomplish them. This is the beauty of math.

Happy journaling!

With gratitude,

Allison and Nicole

> "Whether you believe you can or you can't, you are absolutely right." ~ Henry Ford

How does math make you feel?

Why do you feel this way?

Math is...

FIXED MINDSET	VS	GROWTH MINDSET
• I am bad at math.		• I will improve with practice.
• Math is too hard.		• Math takes time and effort.
• I stick to what I know.		• I try new things.
• I can't do this.		• I can't do this YET.

Which mindset will help you in math: growth mindset or fixed mindset? Why?

Write about a time in math when you said, "I can't do this YET!" and kept practicing?

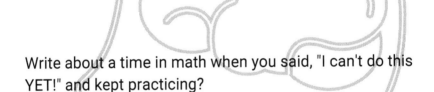

> "If the plan does not work, change the plan, not the goal." ~ unknown

What is a goal you have when you grow up?

What is a goal you have for this year?

How does math help you reach these goals?

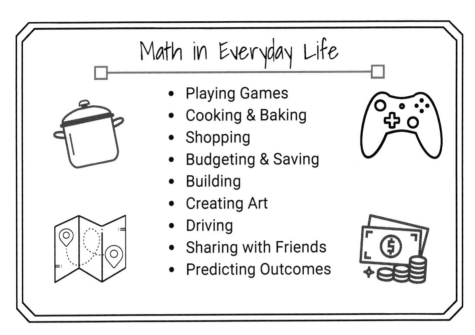

Math in Everyday Life

- Playing Games
- Cooking & Baking
- Shopping
- Budgeting & Saving
- Building
- Creating Art
- Driving
- Sharing with Friends
- Predicting Outcomes

How did you use math in your life today?

What is something you'd like to buy? How can math help you save for it?

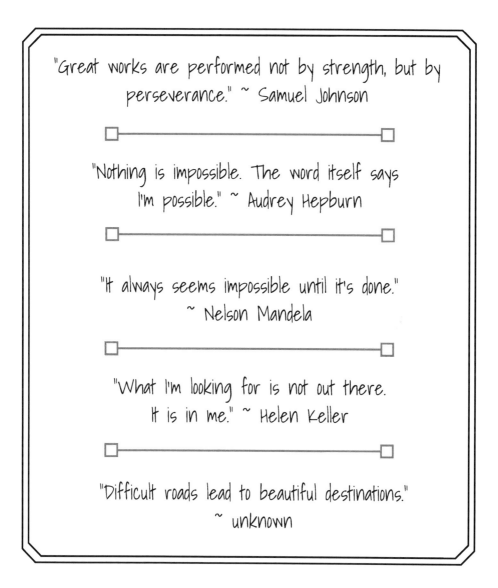

"Great works are performed not by strength, but by perseverance." ~ Samuel Johnson

"Nothing is impossible. The word itself says I'm possible." ~ Audrey Hepburn

"It always seems impossible until it's done." ~ Nelson Mandela

"What I'm looking for is not out there. It is in me." ~ Helen Keller

"Difficult roads lead to beautiful destinations." ~ unknown

A quote that inspires me or calms me when I'm frustrated or have failed is...

Math That's Fun...

Write down a math problem that you had fun solving.

Write down the solution.

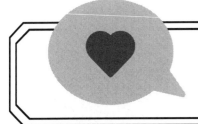

"Do what you love. Love what you do." ~ unknown

What made the problem fun?

What other types of math problems do you find fun?

"You become what you believe."
~ Oprah Winfrey

What are three things you're grateful for?

A challenge I'm thankful that I faced in math is...

"It's not the joy that makes us grateful, it's the gratitude that makes us joyful."
~ David Steindl-Rast

What is Math?

Write down or draw anything that comes to mind.

"Start where you are. Use what you have. Do what you can." ~ Arthur Ashe

> Math is just a skill, just like learning a new language. It require practice, practice, and more practice.

What's a language you have learned or would like to learn?

What did (or will) you need to practice in order to improve?

How can you apply this to math?

> "The future belongs to those who learn more skills and combine them in creative ways."
> ~ Robert Greene

HARD Math Problems

How do you approach hard problems?

When looking at hard problems, ask yourself:
- What is the problem asking?
- What basic skills and strategies will help?
- What information is available to me in the problem?
- What similar problems have I seen and how did I solve those?
- Who can I go to for help?

When solving a hard math problem, what other questions are helpful to ask yourself?

Math That I'm Proud Of...

Write down a hard math problem that you're proud of solving.

Write down the solution.

> "Champions keep playing until they get it right."
> ~ Billy Jean King

> Reflect on your work.

How did you approach this problem?

What basic skills helped you with this problem?

Who did you go to for help if you needed it?

Was there a time when you struggled, got frustrated, or made a mistake? How did you work through that?

> "If you can't measure it, you can't improve it."
> ~ Peter Drucker

It's important to set SMART goals for yourself so you know what it is you're aiming for and can measure your progress toward your goal.

SMART stands for:

S - Specific
M - Measurable
A - Attainable
R - Relevant
T - Timely

Example:
"I will get a B on my math test next week by studying each night this week."

What is a SMART goal that you can set for yourself in math class? (This could refer to the unit you're working on, your next test, your attitude toward math, completing homework, or anything else that you'd like to work toward.)

Check your goal. Is it...

- [ ] Specific?
- [ ] Measurable?
- [ ] Attainable?
- [ ] Relevant?
- [ ] Timely?

Who can help you reach your goal?

How can you check in to make sure you're making progress on your goal?

How will you feel when you reach your goal?

> "Success isn't always about greatness. It's about consistency. Consistent hard work leads to success. Greatness will come."
> ~ Dwayne "The Rock" Johnson

> Think of math as the mental version of soccer. Soccer makes you more fit, stronger, and healthier physically. Math makes you more fit, stronger, and healthier mentally.
> ~ Crush Math Now

What's a sport you play (or would like to learn how to play)?

What skills do you need to practice in order to improve?

What do you do when it gets difficult?

How can you apply this to math?

What are three things you're grateful for?

What is something you learned in math this week that you can celebrate?

"If you see someone without a smile, give them one of yours." ~ Dolly Parton

> "Go down deep enough into anything and you will find mathematics." ~ Dean Schlicter

Whatever you're spending time on, you should know why you're doing it. Why do you need math?

What is something that you are good at in math?

What is a positive experience you've had with math?

What do you hope to learn in math?

"All things are difficult before they are easy."
~ Thomas Fuller

Math That's Fun...

Write down a math problem that you had fun solving.

Write down the solution.

Believe in yourself.

What made the problem fun?

What other types of math problems do you find fun?

"Life is a ticket to the greatest show on earth."
~ Martin H. Fischer

"You must do the things you think you cannot do." ~ Eleanor Roosevelt

What do you think about this quote?

What is something in math you think you cannot do and why is it important to try?

> "Success is the sum of small efforts, repeated day in and day out."
> ~ R. Collier

Good habits set you up for a happy and fulfilled life.
- Going to bed at the same time every night.
- Eating a healthy breakfast.
- Practicing gratitude.
- Being active.

What are some good habits that you have?

Good habits can help you make progress towards your goals in math also.
- Studying flashcards for 5 minutes a day.
- Writing your math homework down in a planner.
- Doing math homework first.

What are some good habits you have for studying math?

> Math is a skill, just like learning a musical instrument. It requires practice and perseverance.

What's a musical instrument you have learned or would like to learn?

What did (or will) you need to practice in order to improve?

How can you apply this to math?

> "Whatever you are, be a good one."
> ~ Abraham Lincoln

What are three things you're grateful for?

What is something you did this week in math that you are proud of?

"Happiness is not something ready-made. It comes from your own actions."
~ Dalai Lama

> If you approach every problem you ever encounter in life with a mathematical mindset, you will solve it. That is the beauty of math. Used correctly, it will elevate your whole life.
> ~ Crush Math Now

Think of ways that you use math in the following areas.

Your health:

Your friendships:

Extra-curricular activities:

Games/Videogames:

> "Success seems to be connected to action. Successful people keep moving. They make mistakes, but they don't quit."
> ~ Conrad Hilton

Who is someone who builds your confidence in math?

What do they say to you?

Write a positive statement to yourself about your abilities in math.

Math That I'm Proud Of...

Write down a hard math problem that you're proud of solving.

Write down the solution.

> Crush the notion that you are "not a math person". There is no such thing as "not a math person". ~ Crush Math Now

> Reflect on your work.

How did you approach this problem?

What basic skills helped you with this problem?

Who did you go to for help if you needed it?

Was there a time when you struggled, got frustrated, or made a mistake? How did you work through that?

> Math is challenging, but did you know that challenges and making mistakes help your brain to grow? Not knowing the answer can be a good thing! The important thing is how you respond to challenges.

Write about a time you overcame a challenge that you were proud of. What did you do to overcome the challenge? How did it make you feel?

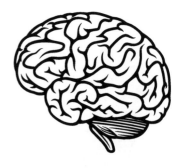

> "The expert at anything was once a beginner." ~ Helen Hayes

How do you feel about asking for help?

What typically happens when you ask for help?

How do you feel when others ask you for help?

What are three things you're grateful for?

How did you use math outside of math class?

"A person who never made a mistake never tried anything new." ~ Albert Einstein

> "Music, mathematics, and art are considered the pinnacle of human creativity." ~ unknown

How do you like to be creative?

Can you find math in your creative outlet?

How is math used in your favorite game?

Math That's Fun...

Write down a math problem that you had fun solving.

Write down the solution.

"Kind words do not cost much. Yet they accomplish much." ~ Blaise Pascal

What made the problem fun?

What other types of math problems do you find fun?

"Find out what your gift is and nurture it."
~ Katy Perry

What does the word CHALLENGE mean to you?

What does your inner voice say during challenging times? What would you like it to say?

> "Great things come from hard work and perseverance. No excuses."
> ~ Kobe Bryant

> Knowing your own strengths and areas of improvement will help you as you face challenging math problems.

What is one of your strengths in math?

What is something you struggle with in math?

What is something you did today that will help you in math tomorrow?

Math and the Five Senses

When you think about math what do you...

see?

hear?

smell?

taste?

feel?

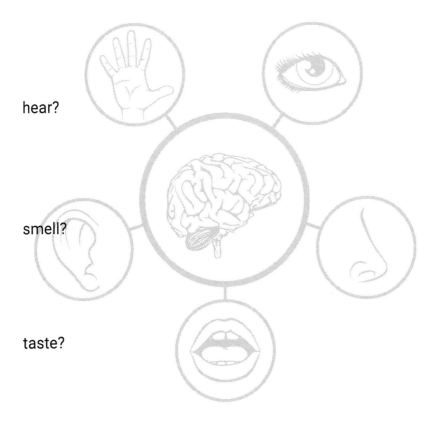

> "The best way to learn is to teach."
> ~ Frank Oppenheimer

What is something you have learned to do that you can teach to someone else?

Who could you teach this to?

How does it feel when you share your knowledge with others?

Math That I'm Proud Of...

Write down a hard math problem that you're proud of solving.

Write down the solution.

> "Be willing to be a beginner every single morning." ~ Meister Eckhart

Reflect on your work.

How did you approach this problem?

What basic skills helped you with this problem?

Who did you go to for help if you needed it?

Was there a time when you struggled, got frustrated, or made a mistake? How did you work through that?

Write about a mistake that you made in math that you can be grateful for because you learned from it.

What is a skill that you have learned that was difficult?

"There is a difference between not knowing, and now knowing YET." ~ Sheila Tobias

Negative self-talk can happen when we get frustrated. What is a negative statement you catch yourself saying about math (I can't do math, I'm bad at math, etc.) and what can you replace it with?

I catch myself saying:

I will replace it with:

How can you change the way you approach a difficult math problem?

M - Mistakes
A - Allow
T - Thinking to
H - Happen

What are three things you're grateful for?

What was the best part of math class this week?

"Don't be pushed by your problems, be led by your dreams." ~ Ralph Waldo Emerson

Who is someone that helps you with math?

How does that person help you?

How does it make you feel when someone helps you?

Talking through math problems with a study buddy can help reinforce concepts and make learning more fun. After all, friends make everything more fun!

Math That's Fun...

Write down a math problem that you had fun solving.

Write down the solution.

> Math will make you a stronger, prouder, smarter, and more capable person.
> ~ Crush Math Now

What made the problem fun?

What other types of math problems do you find fun?

"In a world where you can be anything, be KIND." ~ unknown

What are three things you are grateful to have learned in math?

What tech tools are you grateful for in math?

What is one way that math has made your life easier or better?

"A grateful heart is a magnet for miracles."
~ unknown

> "We are all wired differently and we can all do math." ~ Gina Cherkowski

What is the nicest thing a student or teacher has done for you in math class?

What is the best part about being a math student?

What is your favorite memory about math this year?

> Done is better than perfect.

How could the concept above make math less stressful?

What can you tell yourself when you're overwhelmed with trying to find the right answer?

> "The only way to learn mathematics is to DO mathematics."
> ~ Paul Halmos

> "Good mathematics is not about how many answers you know. It's about how you behave when you don't know." ~ unknown

How does it make you feel when you persevere with a math problem?

What part of learning math is better than you thought it would be?

Math That I'm Proud Of...

Write down a hard math problem that you're proud of solving.

Write down the solution.

> Math will teach you to overcome challenges.
> Math will help you change the world.
> ~ Crush Math Now

Reflect on your work.

How did you approach this problem?

What basic skills helped you with this problem?

Who did you go to for help if you needed it?

Was there a time when you struggled, got frustrated, or made a mistake? How did you work through that?

> "The true sign of intelligence is not knowledge, but imagination." ~ Albert Einstein

What do you think about this quote by Albert Einstein (one of the greatest mathemeticians of all time)?

Write about a time you used your imagination.

How can your imagination help you with math?

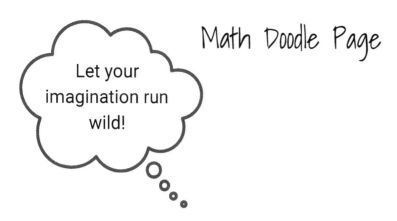

Math Doodle Page

"Everything you can imagine is real."
~ Pablo Picasso

What are three things you're grateful for?

There is no fairy godmother who will wave a magic wand, and make math easy. Why is this a good thing?

"The true measure of success is how many times you bounce back from failure."
~ Stephen Richards

> "Mistakes are proof that you are trying."
> ~ unknown

What are some basic math skills you *have learned* that help you in math class?

What are some basic math skills that you *can learn* that will help you in math class?

Math That's Fun...

Write down a math problem that you had fun solving.

Write down the solution.

"Mathematics is the music of reason."
~ James Joseph Sylvester

What made the problem fun?

What other types of math problems do you find fun?

"There is no substitute for hard work."
~ Thomas Edison

> "By failing to prepare, you are preparing to fail." ~ Benjamin Franklin

What is your goal for your next math test?

What actions will you take to reach that goal?

> "The only person you should strive to be better than is the person you were yesterday." ~ Matty Mullin

Where is your favorite place to work on math? What makes this place special?

Is there a song that helps you relax or think about things you're grateful for?

What is something that cheers you up when you're feeling down?

What is a positive experience you have had in math class?

What is something you look forward to in math?

Who encouraged you this week in math?

Math: the only place where people can buy 64 watermelons and no one wonders why.

> "Education is the most powerful weapon which you can use to change the world."
> ~ Nelson Mandela

What is something you use everyday that you're grateful for and why?

What is your favorite math website and how is it helpful?

Math That I'm Proud Of...

Write down a hard math problem that you're proud of solving.

Write down the solution.

"Everyone makes mistakes. That's why pencils have erasers." ~ Japanese proverb

Reflect on your work.

How did you approach this problem?

What basic skills helped you with this problem?

Who did you go to for help if you needed it?

Was there a time when you struggled, got frustrated, or made a mistake? How did you work through that?

Strategies for Coping with Anxiety

- Practice self-care
- Meditate
- Do something creative
- Exercise/Play a sport
- Sleep
- Practice deep breathing
- Talk to someone you trust
- Ask for help
- Take a break
- Listen to music

Which of the above strategies have you tried before?

Which strategies would you like to try?

What is something you can do when you are feeling anxious?

What is your favorite way to relax?

"Almost anything will work again if you unplug it for a few minutes... including you."
~ Anne Lamott

"One of the secrets of life is that all that is really worth doing is what we do for others."
~ Lewis Carroll

Who is a math teacher, tutor or friend you are grateful for?

What is a compliment you could give your math teacher, tutor, or friend?

What are three things you're grateful for?

What is something you've done that makes you proud?

"Nothing is a mistake. There's no win and no fail. There's only make." ~ Corita Kent

> "Do the best you can until you know better. Then when you know better, do better."
> ~ Maya Angelou

Think of a time when you did something difficult and wanted to give up. What did you do to persevere?

When was a time you asked a question about math and it helped?

> "The man on top of the mountain didn't fall there." ~ Vince Lombardi

How does math make you feel?

Why do you feel this way?

Math is...

How has your mindset about math changed?

What changes have you made to how you do math?

"Mathematics gives us hope that every problem has a solution." ~ unknown

What is a concept that you have learned that was difficult?

What accomplishment, big or small, are you proud of?

"Doubt kills more dreams than failure every will."
~ Suzy Kassem

My Fun & Challenging Math Problems

Use the following pages to showcase different math problems you've solved this year. You can highlight fun problems that you enjoyed and challenging problems you're proud of.

Problem #1

> "You have not failed until you quit trying."
> ~ Gordon B. Hinckley

Problem #2

> "Courage is like a muscle - we strengthen it by use." ~ Ruth Gordon

Problem #3

"How you climb a mountain is more important than reaching the top." ~ Yvon Chouinard

Problem #4

"One finds limits by pushing them."
~ Herbert Simon

Problem #5

"Discipline is the bridge between goals and accomplishment." ~ Jim Rohn

Problem #6

"Today, fill your cup of life with sunshine and laughter." ~ Dodinksy

Problem #7

> "Don't be afraid to fail. Be afraid not to try."
> ~ Michael Jordan

Problem #8

"Math doesn't get easier.
You get stronger." ~ Crush Math Now

Problem #9

"Stay positive. Work hard. Make it happen."
~ unknown

Problem #10

> "The struggle ends when gratitude begins."
> ~ Neale Donald Walsch

Special Thanks

Allison
To Joe, for your endless support and encouragement.
To the kids, for giving me the time and space to work on this fun project!

Nicole
To Kyle, for being an inspiring leader and spreading joy throughout your entire school community.
To the kids, for your curiosity and love of learning.

About the Author - Allison Dillard

Allison Dillard is a math professor, host of the *Allison Loves Math Podcast* and author of the Amazon bestselling book, *Crush Math Now*. She has an M.S. in Mathematics from Claremont Graduate University and a B.A. in English and a B.A. in Mathematics from Scripps College.

When she's not teaching or writing, you'll find her playing board games with her awesome husband, coaching her kids' soccer teams or dreaming up new ways to convince the world that math is awesome. Her love for math is legendary.

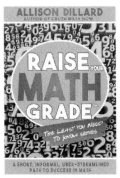

You can get a free copy of Allison's book, *Raise Your Math Grade*, at www.allisonlovesmath.com/freebook.

About the Author - Nicole Thomson

Nicole Thomson spent over a decade teaching in the elementary school system where she was involved in action research projects, including Math 4 Young Children. She has an M. Ed from Charles Sturt University, an H.B. Comm, and B. Ed from Lakehead University and is now an Academic Upgrading professor.

Nicole founded *The Fulfilled Classroom* to inspire educators to live life with gratitude, joy, and intention, both in and out of the classroom. She has also written her first children's book, *"The Little Things: Finding Gratitude in Life's Simple Moments"*. Nicole lives in Northern Ontario, Canada with her husband and two children.

To try out your own gratitude practice at home or in the classroom, you can sign up for 30 Days of Gratitude Prompts for free at www.thefulfilledclassroom.com/resources.

FREE Guide for Teachers and Parents

For a quick, step-by-step guide to introduce this resource to your class or children, go to www.allisonlovesmath.com/journal.

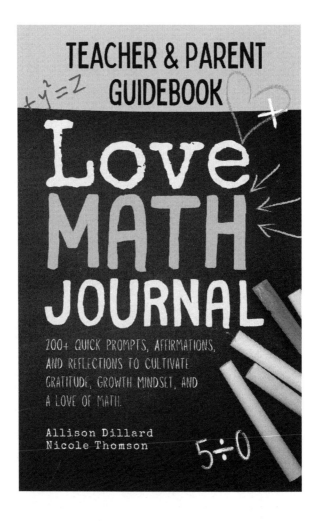

Made in the USA
Columbia, SC
29 June 2021